Loud Speakers
for God

Keith McCullough

Illustrated by Beccy Blake

By the same author:
Travellers' Tales
Mighty Warriors for God

© Keith McCullough 2003

First published 2003

Cover design: Nick Ward
Illustrations: Beccy Blake

Scripture Union, 207–209 Queensway, Bletchley,
Milton Keynes, MK2 2EB, England.
Email: info@scriptureunion.org.uk
Website: www.scriptureunion.org.uk

ISBN 1 85999 557 8

British Library Cataloguing-in-Publication Data.
A catalogue record of this book is available from the
British Library.

Printed and bound in Great Britain by
Creative Print and Design (Wales) Ebbw Vale.

ℰ *Scripture Union is an international Christian charity working with churches
in more than 130 countries, providing resources to bring the good news about
Jesus Christ to children, young people and families and to encourage them to
develop spiritually through the Bible and prayer.*

*As well as our network of volunteers, staff and associates who run holidays,
church-based events and school Christian groups, we produce a wide range of
publications and support those who use our resources through training
programmes.*

Introduction

God speaks to us in many wonderful ways.

He speaks of his great power through the things he has made.

He speaks of his great promises through the Bible.

He speaks of his great love through his son, Jesus.

But there is a special group of people who hear his voice and pass on his message.

They are called prophets.

They are loud speakers for God.

You can read all about them in this book!

Contents

Elijah

The fiery prophet

Elijah pushed aside the guards who were standing before the great doors to the throne room and marched straight up to the king. There sat King Ahab and Queen Jezebel on their golden thrones. Elijah's eyes blazed as he glared at the royal couple.

There will be no more rain!

Having delivered his message Elijah stormed out of the palace.

God was very angry with the people of Israel because they had broken their promise to worship him only. They had chosen to worship another god called Baal.

God was very angry with Queen Jezebel because she had brought Baal-worship to Israel when she married the king.

God was very angry with King Ahab because he had built a temple to Baal in his main city.

Baal was supposed to be a weather god who could send rain and sun, thunder and lightning. So if the people wanted good weather they prayed to him.

Oh Baal! Give me a good harvest!

But Baal was not real. He was just an idol made of stone. He had no power at all.

God *was* real. He had power to control the weather. So he decided to punish the people and teach them a lesson. He decided to stop sending any more rain for three long years.

As the months passed the rivers dried up, the grass burnt up and a fierce sun scorched the earth from out of a cloudless sky. Crops withered, animals died and the people began to get very hungry.

After three years, Elijah came back to King Ahab.

Once more he stood before the king.

"Call the prophets of Baal and call all the people," he thundered. "Tell them to gather at the top of

Mount Carmel and I'll meet them
there. We will have a contest to see
whether the God of Israel or Baal is
the true god."

The prophets of Baal, the people of
Israel and King Ahab all came together
as Elijah had commanded. Then the
prophet challenged the people.

Elijah turned to the prophets of Baal.
"Build an altar with these rocks. Put
firewood on it. Kill a bull as a sacrifice
and put it on the firewood. Then call
on Baal to send down fire from heaven

to burn everything up. I will do the same. The god who sends the fire will be god!"

The prophets of Baal agreed. They built their altar. They put their bull on the wood. Then they danced in a circle round the altar calling to their god.

The people watched and waited for something to happen.

Nothing did.

Hour after hour the prophets of Baal called on their god. They chanted, they danced, they cut themselves with knives until the blood spurted out.

"Send your fire!" they screamed.

Nothing happened.

Elijah teased them. "Call louder!" he laughed. "Perhaps Baal is asleep – maybe he's gone on a journey!"

In the end the Baal prophets gave up, exhausted. They had failed.

In a gentle voice Elijah called the people to gather round. He had already built his altar and put the sacrifice ready. Suddenly, he made a very strange request.

"Fill four large water jars with water from the sea," he said.

Meanwhile he dug a trench around the altar. When the men returned he poured the buckets of water over the sacrifice until everything was soaked. Then he asked for more water, and more. The people watched, astonished.

Elijah prayed, "Lord God of Abraham, Isaac and Jacob, let it be known today that you are the real God of Israel."

With a mighty roar the fire fell from heaven. It burnt up everything, even the rocks of the altar.

The people realised that Elijah's God was the *real* God.

"Now God will send you rain," promised Elijah.

You can find this story in 1 Kings chapter 17 verse 1 and chapter 18 verses 16–46.

Elisha

The room on the roof

The baby was perfect, even down to his
smallest fingernail. He was a wonderful
gift from God. The baby's mother held
him tightly and smiled at her husband.

"Elisha spoke the truth," she said. "He promised that we would have a son."

"God has rewarded you for your kindness," replied her husband.

She had been very kind to Elisha the prophet. Whenever he had passed their house on a journey, she had invited him inside for a meal. She had had a small room built on the flat roof of her house where he could spend the night. There were stairs built on the wall of the house to get to the room. She had even put a bed, a table, a chair and an oil lamp in the room. It was very comfortable.

In return, Elisha had promised that God would give her what she wanted most of all – a son. Now she would have someone to take care of her when she was old.

The little boy grew quickly. He was healthy and strong. He loved to help his father on the farm.

"It will soon be harvest time again," said his father cheerfully.

Father and son stood watching the golden corn blowing in the wind.

"One day all this will be yours."

It was time to cut the corn. Father and some of his neighbours went into the field armed with sharp, curved knives. His son and some of the village boys followed to tie the fallen corn into bundles. It was very hard work and the sun was very hot.

"Take him to his mother!" the father ordered his servant.

The servant picked up the boy and carried him to the house.

Mother sat him on her lap and rocked him gently back and forth. He looked so ill. What could she do?

The boy moaned once or twice and then he just stopped breathing.

He had died. It was a terrible thing to happen.

The mother held her son in her arms for a long time. She was still sitting there when her husband came home for dinner.

Together they carried him up the stairs and laid him on the prophet's bed.

Elisha shaded his eyes against the sun and looked into the distance.

"There is someone coming to see us," he said to his servant. "I can see a man leading a donkey with someone on it."

As she drew nearer Elisha recognised her. "It's the woman from Shunem. Go and greet her and ask if all is well with her family."

The woman came up to Elisha and threw herself at his feet. She was crying.

"What's the matter?" he asked.

"God gave me a son and God has taken him back again," she replied. "Please help me!"

Elisha and his servant walked back with her to the village.

When they reached the house Elisha went up to his room on the roof and saw the boy lying on the bed. He ordered everybody out of the room, closed the door and began to pray.

"O Lord God! Give this boy back his life," he prayed.

Then he climbed onto the bed on top of the boy. He lay mouth to mouth, eyes to eyes, hands to hands and continued to pray.

Gradually the boy's body grew warm.

The prophet walked backwards and forwards across the room then stretched himself on the boy again.

Suddenly the boy sneezed seven times and opened his eyes!

Elisha called his servant who had been waiting outside the door. "Tell the boy's mother to come here," he told him.

She climbed the stairs and looked with wonder through the open door. Her son was sitting on the bed smiling at her!

"Here he is, safe and sound," said Elisha, smiling. "Take him downstairs and give him something to eat."

"Thank you, man of God," she exclaimed joyfully.

"It is God you must thank," Elisha replied.

You can find this story in 2 Kings chapter 4 verses 8–37.

Jonah

The second chance

One minute the sea had been calm, the next a great storm arose out of nowhere.

The wind screamed through the sails and the great ship was tossed about like a cork in the ocean.

Everyone was praying to their own gods. They even threw their cargo overboard to try and save the ship.

"Someone on this ship has made his god angry," said the captain. "So we are all being punished. Let's find out who it is."

The sailors put each person's name on a stick and dropped the sticks into a bucket.

"The name that we pull out is the one who's to blame," they agreed.

It was Jonah.

The sea grew rougher still and the sailors grew more terrified.

Jonah stood before the frightened men.

"Who are you? Where do you come from? What are you doing here?" The questions rained down upon Jonah like the storm.

"I'm running away from my God," Jonah exclaimed. "He wants me to go to Nineveh and I don't want to go. Throw me into the sea and the storm will stop," he promised.

The sailors tried and tried to get the ship back to port but the storm got

stronger and stronger. They prayed to
Jonah's God, picked him up and threw
him overboard.

As soon as Jonah's body hit the water,
everything went calm.

Jonah sank to the bottom of the sea.
He was afraid he was going to drown
but he didn't. Instead a huge fish
appeared. It opened its mouth wide and,
with one gulp, swallowed Jonah whole!

Jonah found himself inside the fish's
slimy tummy. He was cold and wet and
very uncomfortable but he was alive.

"Thank you, Lord, for saving me,"
he murmured.

Jonah pulled the seaweed out of his
hair and beard. He found a lump of
something soft to sit on.

It was pitch dark in there and the
fish's tummy smelled awful. He could
feel the fish moving as it swam strongly
through the sea and he could hear its
heart beating like a big bass drum.
Thump! Thump! Thump!

"I wonder where we are going?" he
asked himself. Then he started to pray.

"Please give me another chance," he continued. "I will do whatever you ask, I promise. But please rescue me from this terrible place."

When he had finished praying Jonah felt quite peaceful. He was sure God had heard his prayers. He knew God would rescue him. And he guessed that God had sent the fish to bring him home.

Suddenly the fish was sick and Jonah was thrown out onto the beach. He was right back where he had started. He had been inside the fish for three days.

This time Jonah headed for Nineveh. He had to walk 500 miles!

While he walked, Jonah had time to think about what he would say. The people of Nineveh were wicked, and they hated God and his ways. Jonah felt they should be punished. Well, it would serve them right! But God had a different idea.

Jonah marched into the city. The crowd, seeing a foreigner in their city, gathered round him.

Jonah spoke in a loud voice. "God has sent me to tell you that in forty days he is going to destroy your city."

Jonah expected the people to laugh, but they were terrified.

News soon reached the king and he ordered everybody to stop all the wrong things they were doing and show how sorry they were.

"Put on sacks!" he ordered. "Sit down in the dust! Go without food or drink! Pray for forgiveness! Perhaps Jonah's God will show mercy."

Jonah waited outside the city to see what God would do.

Forty days passed and the city was still there. The people were so relieved. God had heard their prayers and forgiven them.

Jonah was so angry. Is God just going to forgive them, he thought, after all I've been through?

"I knew you wouldn't destroy them," Jonah complained angrily. "That's why I didn't want to come here in the first place."

God provided shade for his prophet. A bush grew with broad leaves to protect Jonah's head from the sun.

But the next day, a little worm bit through the plant and destroyed it. Jonah missed its shade and protection.

"Why did you do that, God?" he asked.

"Jonah!" said God. "You care a lot about a plant, but you don't care about the thousands of people in Nineveh. Don't be angry anymore – I love the people of Nineveh."

You can find this story in the book of Jonah.

Isaiah

The call

"The king is dead!"

For over 50 years the king had reigned in the land of Judah. Now his son would reign over them, but what kind of king would he be? Would he be good and faithful?

Isaiah thought about the death of the king. He went into the Temple to pray. It was a wonderful building, built by King Solomon many years ago. It was called the house of prayer because there the Holy God of Israel would meet with his people.

Isaiah stood by the great stone altar, where the fire for the evening sacrifice was still glowing red. It was quiet in

the Temple court and Isaiah prayed to
the God of Israel.

As Isaiah opened his eyes he saw a
glorious sight.

He saw a huge throne standing in the
entrance to the most special place in the
Temple. Seated on the throne he saw
God himself. He was dressed like a great
king and his long robes filled the Temple.
His face shone brighter than the sun.

Then Isaiah heard the sweetest music
and, looking up, he saw creatures from
heaven flying in circles above the

throne. The creatures sang as they worshipped God.

Isaiah stood amazed at this marvellous sight. He thought he was looking into heaven itself.

The music grew louder as Isaiah felt God all around him and the glory of God's presence grew brighter. Then the ground started shaking beneath his feet. The whole Temple seemed to move as though there was an earthquake and the whole place was filled with smoke.

Isaiah was so frightened that he fell flat on his face. He was sure he was going to die!

But Isaiah didn't die. Instead one of the creatures reached down and picked up a piece of glowing wood from the altar. He touched Isaiah's lips with it and said, "Now you are clean. Use your lips to bring glory to God."

Isaiah was amazed. The fire didn't hurt a bit. In fact it was as sweet as honey. And he didn't feel afraid any more.

Isaiah looked up into the blazing light of God's presence. The Lord spoke to him with a voice of thunder.

God said to Isaiah, "Go to all the cities and villages of the land. Tell them that the God of Israel is their king. Tell them what you have seen and heard. But they won't listen to you. They won't see what you have seen.

Even so, you must keep speaking to them. The time will come when they will *have* to listen!"

So Isaiah's life as a prophet began. God shared many wonderful secrets with him. Perhaps the most exciting one was that, one day, God would visit the earth he had made. He would come as a little baby and his name would be Immanuel, which means God is with us.

We call that baby JESUS!

You can find this story in Isaiah chapter 6.

Jeremiah

The pen and the knife

"God is speaking again," Jeremiah
called to his friend Baruch.

Baruch got hold of a scroll, a pen and some ink and waited for Jeremiah to begin. Jeremiah began. "This is what the Lord God of Israel says: 'I am going to punish the people of Israel because they have turned their backs on me. They have done wicked things. They have stolen, they have murdered and they have started to worship other gods.'"

Baruch wrote it all down.

"Now go to the Temple," Jeremiah said. "Read it out to all the people."

Baruch went to the Temple and read out the words of the Lord. When the king got to hear of it he sent a message to Baruch.

"Bring the scroll to me. I want to see it for myself."

Baruch brought the scroll to the king, who was sitting in front of a great fire. As the king read the scroll he took out his penknife and cut the scroll into pieces. Then he threw the pieces, one by one, into the fire. His face was dark with anger.

Baruch was horrified. The king had destroyed God's word!

Baruch bowed himself out of the room and reported back to Jeremiah.

"We will start again," said Jeremiah. "Take a pen and write: 'This is what the Lord says...'"

When they had finished Jeremiah added a bit more. "God says to the king, 'Because you have destroyed my word, the King of Babylon will surely destroy you.'"

And that's exactly what happened.
There was a new king but he wasn't
any better. The new king just did what
his officers told him.

"We must stop the prophet from
speaking," they advised. "He is
frightening the people."

So they took Jeremiah and threw him
into a deep, dark well. There was no
water in the well and Jeremiah sank to
his waist in thick, slimy mud.

Poor Jeremiah! He couldn't help but feel sorry for himself. Then he remembered the promise God had made when he first called him to be a prophet. "Don't be afraid of them, for I am with you and I will rescue you." So he waited patiently to be rescued. He did not have long to wait.

There was a man in the king's service who came from Sudan. His name was Ebedmelech. Plucking up his courage, he went to the king and begged him to let Jeremiah go.

"You have my permission to pull the prisoner out," the king said. "Take some men with you and some ropes."

Ebedmelech chose thirty men and gathered together a pile of old clothes. He went to the well and dropped the clothes over the edge.

"Put these rags under your armpits," he said. "They will protect you against the ropes. We are going to pull you out."

Jeremiah did as he was told and the tug-of-war began.

As the men heaved on the ropes, thick, sticky mud pulled back at Jeremiah's body. It seemed to take forever when suddenly the mud let go and Jeremiah was lifted to safety.

You can find this story in Jeremiah chapter 36 to chapter 38 verse 13.

Ezekiel

The valley of bones

"Ezekiel – follow me!" The voice was quite clear. It was the voice of God.

So Ezekiel followed God into a great valley between the mountains. It was a scary place. Ezekiel walked up and down a valley that was full of bones. As far as he could see there were human bones scattered all over the ground. There were leg bones, backbones and grinning skulls. They were bleached white by the desert sun and they were very, very dry.

Ezekiel shook his head at the question. "You know best, Lord," he replied.

"Speak to the bones!" God commanded. "Tell them the words that I shall give to you."

Ezekiel felt a bit foolish but he did what he was told.

"Dry bones!" he shouted. "Hear the word of the Lord!"

His voice echoed around the valley. "Hear the word of the Lord! Hear the word of the Lord!"

Then there was complete silence. Ezekiel tried again.

"Dry bones! Listen to me. This is what the Lord says. 'I will make you live again. I will join you together. I will put skin on you. I will breathe on you and you will live.'"

Ezekiel expected to hear the echo again but before he'd even finished speaking the bones began to move towards each other.

Ezekiel stared in astonishment and fear.

Next a rattling sound broke the silence. The noise grew and grew as the bones found their partners and joined together.

Ezekiel watched in wonder as leg bones joined backbones, arm bones joined shoulder bones and neck bones joined grinning skulls. Soon there were complete skeletons lying on the ground.

The skeletons were slowly covered with muscles and skin. The skulls were covered with hair, ears and eyes. Lips and noses appeared on their faces. Soon there were human bodies lying all around. But they weren't alive.

Then God said to Ezekiel, "Call to the winds! Tell them to come and breathe into these bodies."

So Ezekiel called out to the four winds.

"Winds of the north, of the south, of the east and of the west. Listen to the word of the Lord!"

"The word of the Lord! The word of the Lord!" the echo repeated.

Then the winds began to blow. They howled through the valley. Ezekiel's hair and clothes were blowing wildly. He was nearly swept away by the force of the gale!

The bodies began to move as the breath of life filled them. Then they sat up. Then they stood up. Next they started walking about and shouting with joy.

Ezekiel watched amazed as this great crowd of people leapt about praising God.

"Now! Go to my people Israel," commanded God. "Tell them what you have seen."

The people of Israel were far away. They were living in a foreign land where they had been taken as prisoners. They were forced to do hard work and were beaten and given hardly any food to eat.

When Ezekiel came to them they stood before him in their rags.

Now Ezekiel understood why God had shown him the dry bones. Just as he had put new life into the bones, so God could give new life to his people.

"God is going to gather you together and bring you home," he promised. "He is going to breathe on you and fill you with his Spirit. He is going to bring you back to life. God is in control and he will do it."

For the first time in many years the people smiled. Already they could feel new hope in their hearts.

"The Lord is God!" they said.

You can find this story in Ezekiel chapter 37 verses 1–14.

Simeon and Anna

How long?

"How long, O Lord? How long do we have to wait for the Christ, your chosen one?"

Every day Simeon fell on his knees and cried to God. As he waited in silence after his prayer, God spoke to him.

Simeon! You will live to see the Christ.

Simeon was thrilled. He was an old man and he would surely die soon. But he believed God.

There was someone else in the great Temple in Jerusalem. Her name was Anna and she was a prophetess. She was eighty-four years old but that did not stop her getting out of bed every day at sunrise and spending the day in the Temple. She was well known by all the Temple priests and staff, for she had been there for as long as anyone could remember.

Anna spent her days worshipping God and praying. She went without food all day as well so that she could concentrate on God. Anna also walked up to all the parents who brought their babies into the Temple.

Anna was looking forward to the time when God would send his son into the world.

One day God said to Simeon, "I want you to go to the Temple now."

Simeon had learned to obey God, so he went straight away. And what a good thing he did, for at that very time Joseph and Mary were coming into the Temple.

Mary was carrying Jesus in her arms. He was just forty days old and the time had come to present him to God as the law required. Joseph was carrying two pigeons in a little wooden cage to give thanks for the child.

The Spirit of God said to Simeon, "Here is the Saviour of the world."

Simeon's face shone with joy.

"Please may I hold your baby?" he asked as he walked towards them.

Thank you, Lord. Now I'm ready.

Then Simeon gave Mary and Joseph his blessing.

At that very moment Anna came forward. She had heard Simeon's words and she wanted to see the baby too.

A toothless smile cracked her wrinkled face as she looked closely into the face of Jesus. Jesus smiled back at her, his big eyes fixed on her face.

Mary and Joseph marvelled at this magic moment. Then Simeon spoke again.

"This child will bring great joy to those who believe in him and great sorrow to those who don't believe. But he will suffer, and so will you."

As Simeon spoke these words, he looked straight at Mary. She wondered what lay ahead.

But the dark cloud passed instantly as Anna brought people to see Jesus.

"Come and see," she invited the people. "Come and see the one who will grow up to save his people."

You can find this story in Luke chapter 2 verses 22–38.

John the Baptist

Preparing the way

God's special prophets from long ago said he would come. They were right! He came storming out of the desert like another Elijah.

"Get ready! God's kingdom is coming!" he thundered.

He was fierce and fearless and he even told the king off for his bad behaviour, just like Elijah did many years before him. His name was John the Baptist. God had called John to prepare the people for the coming of Jesus.

John stood on the banks of the river and challenged everybody who came to listen to him.

"You must change your ways," he said. "You must say 'Sorry!' for the things you have done wrong. Be baptised as a sign that you want your old ways washed away."

The people stepped into the river up to their waists and John ducked them under the water.

"Now you are clean," declared John. "Don't do wrong anymore."

"What shall we do now?" the crowd asked John.

"Share your food and clothes with people who don't have any," John replied. "Be honest in your business and be happy with what you have."

John had enemies. He saw them coming. They were the leaders in

Jerusalem and they thought they were better than ordinary people. But John was not afraid of them. He pointed a finger at them.

"You are like snakes," he shouted. "But the fire of God's anger will burn you up. You can't escape."

"You are like fruit trees that don't produce fruit," he continued. "But the axe of God's anger will chop you down and throw you on the fire."

His enemies went away muttering angrily.

When the crowd had been baptised John spoke to them again.

"There is a great man coming. I'm not good enough even to carry his sandals. I have baptised you with water to show your sins can be forgiven. But he will baptise people with the Holy Spirit's power. Be prepared, for he is coming soon!"

Even as he spoke, a man stepped out of the crowd and walked towards John the Baptist. John knew him instantly.

"Baptise me, John," said Jesus.

"No! How can you ask me?" replied John. "I need to be baptised by *you*."

"It is right to do as God asks," Jesus said gently but firmly.

So John led Jesus into the water and Jesus was baptised as an example to all the people. As soon as he came up out of the water, the people saw and heard something so wonderful that they would never forget it.

This is my son.
I love him and
I am pleased with
him.

John's work was done. Jesus had come.

John was content to step back into the crowd. From now on all eyes were on Jesus.

You can find this story in Matthew chapter 3.

If you've enjoyed this book, why not
look out for…

By the same author:
Mighty Warriors For God
Keith McCullough

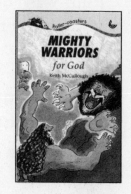

"If I catch David I'll kill
him," declared King Saul.
  But David is fearless and
creeps into Saul's camp at
night with his nephew
Abishai… what will they do when they finally
have the king at their mercy?
  David wasn't the only man to go into battle
for God – meet some famous and less well
known fighters in the Bible and discover what
it takes to be a warrior for God.

ISBN 1 85999 557 8

Angel Alert!
Brian Ogden

King Nebuchadnezzar flew
into a right royal rage because
the three friends would not
bow down to his statue. He
had them tied up and thrown
into a furnace. As he looked
on, the king was amazed. "Didn't we throw
three men into the fire? Then why are there
four men now? The fourth one looks like an
angel!" he exclaimed.

Exciting and strange stories from the Bible
about angels who were sent by God to help
his people.

ISBN 1 85999 494 6

Food, Glorious Food!
Barbara Smith

The boy looked at Jesus' face
and thought, I can't eat all
this myself, when other
people are hungry. After that
it was amazing. There was
enough food for everyone!

  Read about Moses, Elijah, Abigail, Daniel
and others who discovered that God was
interested in food too.

ISBN 1 85999 477 6

*All of these titles are available from
Christian bookshops, or online at
www.scriptureunion.org.uk/publishing or
call Mail Order direct on 01908 856006.*